Welc

Fellow Parents and Guardian Angels,
Thank You For Your Purchase!

Allow me to introduce myself, my name is Orite Levy, owner and curator/designer of,
Assorted Arts Press Kids!.
&
Assorted Arts Press

Not only am I a strong small business owner but a proud single mother of
a growing son and full time caretaker for my 95yo gran.
As you can see, family is important to me and so are our children.
It is my goal to make quality books for all kids and as a parent who has homeschooled for
years, i feel I have a handle on what works well and is worth while, however,
I would LOVE your feedback,

GIVE ME YOUR THOUGHTS!

!!Bonus!!

**I am in need of reviews to boost this budding business, If you love this book and leave a
5 star written review, take a screen shot of your submitted review and send it to the email
below, I will send you a free downloadable positive affirmation coloring book! :)**

If you have anything other than a five star review, feel free to leave it if you feel the need
and also, I would ask for your personal feedback instead as poor reviews are damaging..
Please contact me letting me know what YOU would
change to make this book even better.
Or, tell me what it is that you think needs adjusting. I am open to
YOUR outside perspective and welcome it!
Let me hear your voices!

Happily raving reviews always welcome... ☺
It takes a community and I am glad to have you as a part of ours.

Direct all comments to Assortedartspress@gmail.com
Include the book you are referencing.
Thanks!

Student Information:

Year: ....

Age: ....

Grade: ....

For all of our other books scan the QR code below

SCAN ME

A note to the Adults:

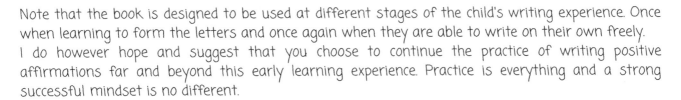

Hello Fellow Adults,

Thank you for choosing this book for your growing young minds.
By choosing this book you are setting your children up for success.

Note that the book is designed to be used at different stages of the child's writing experience. Once when learning to form the letters and once again when they are able to write on their own freely.
I do however hope and suggest that you choose to continue the practice of writing positive affirmations far and beyond this early learning experience. Practice is everything and a strong successful mindset is no different.

When this book is used regularly, or other affirmation practices, you may notice your child walking around talking to themselves in a very different, more uplifting way. This is the beginning of a new way of thinking about themselves and how they take on the situations in their lives. This world can be a very negative place and so can the set of our own minds become quite negative,, so why not start the positive mindset training young? Empower your children to overcome life's challenges and rise to the top by feeling confident and worthy, strong enough to reach their goals/dreams. i know I want that for my son.

In this book you will find big words, maybe even strange words, all words have a definition and it is never too early to learn big words. These kiddos are sponges and learn what we teach no matter the age. Make sure to discuss the definitions, ask them for examples and then provide more examples and more clarity so that they fully understand and adapt the word they are working on.

One of my fondest memories from the age of three, was the accomplishment that I felt at being able to spell the word "Beautiful" it was a "BIG" word. I felt beautiful because I was told what it meant and that i was beautiful inside and out. I was so proud of myself for this new "BIG" knowledge, so do not underestimate your children, they are quick to learn with repetition and explanation of definition and are hungry for it.

Another important impression to make is that practice is what gets us to our goals and taking daily action, such as tracing/writing daily will create an outcome, in this case, it is much better penmanship. All cases differ depending on what is being practiced. This style of daily action is setting kids up for successful life habits, for balance and for good mental wellbeing.

Lastly, children learn best by example, so maybe , just maybe, it wouldn't be a bad idea to add I AM Affirmations to your own daily practices. You may find yourself walking around talking to yourself in a very different, more uplifting way. ;)

Thank you for your support and for supporting young minds everywhere!

Message to the Kiddos,

(Adult please read to child and translate when needed, make sure the child has a good understanding of this page before beginning the practice.)

Welcome to your positive affirmation practice, this is a practice to be done daily and as much as possible throughout your whole life.
When you do these practices over and over throughout your life, you will build a strong base for all your successes and will be even MORE likely to reach your dreams!
Congratulations to you for making yourself a stronger more successful human being!
Remember this, feeling is everything when saying and learning positive affirmations and for now, one word a day is perfect.
It is important to believe these affirmations with all your heart. To feel as if you actually are what you are affirming because, YOU ARE!
Understand that sometimes in life you will experience people who do not see or understand your dreams and that is o.k. They will likely unintentionally tell you "you can't" and this is just not true.
It may be true for them but only YOU know your own truth!
You have the power to create anything you put your mind, heart and actions toward and it is up to you to disregard the disbelief of others.
Remember not to judge them, they may not realize that they are expressing a limited view and they just can't see beyond their own limits.

You are limitless!!

So, every time you practice in this book make sure you say the affirmation aloud with feelings of joy and empowerment because you are Brilliant, Awesome, Talented and so much more!
You CAN and will succeed at reaching your dreams if you continue to take action toward them everyday in some way and believe first in yourself and not in what others tell you you can or can not accomplish.
You are a shining star, shine baby!

What does your unicorn look like? Draw its face on the opposite page. ⟶

Unicorns come in all
types, just like people
and we all LOVE to
dance!

a b c d e f g

h i j k l m n o

p q r s t u v

w x y z

MY FAMILY

Draw a picture of your family and label them. Be sure to include any pets you have!

MY HOME

Draw a picture of your house from the front. Include trees, pets and all the things you see when you come home.

Draw yourself being amazing.

A a = Amazing - To be surprisingly wonderful. Stunningly impressive.

I am amazing!

I am amazing!

I am amazing!

You try it now...

I am amazing!

I am amazing!

I am amazing!

I am amazing!

I am amazing!

I am amazing!

I am amazing!

You try it now...

One Step Up: You Write It!

I am amazing!

I am amazing!

Draw yourself being brave.

Adult read to child: B b = Brave - Ready to face anything life brings your way. Showing much courage.

I am brave!

I am brave!

I am brave!

You try it now...

I am brave.

I am brave.

I am brave.

I am brave.

I am brave.

I am brave.

I am brave.

You try it now...

One Step Up: You Write It!

I am brave!

I am brave!

Draw yourself being clever.

Adult read to chilld: C c = Clever - Quick to understand things. Quick to learn and apply ideas to life.

I am clever!

I am clever!

I am clever!

You try it now...

I am clever!

I am clever!

I am clever!

I am clever!

I am clever!

I am clever!

I am clever!

You try it now...

One Step Up: You Write It!

I am clever!

I am clever!

Draw something delightful.

I am delightful!

I am delightful!

I am delightful!

You try it now...

I am delightful!

I am delightful!

I am delightful!

I am delightful!

I am delightful!

I am delightful!

I am delightful!

You try it now...

One Step Up: You Write It!

I am delightful!

I am delightful!

Draw yourself being efficient.

I am efficient!

I am efficient!

I am efficient!

You try it now...

I am efficient!

I am efficient!

I am efficient!

I am efficient!

I am efficient!

I am efficient!

I am efficient!

You try it now…

One Step Up: You Write It!

I am efficient!

I am efficient!

Draw yourself being fearless.

Adult read to chilld: F f = Fearless - Without fear, someone who is not afraid and goes after what they want.

I am fearless!

I am fearless!

I am fearless!

You try it now...

I am fearless!

I am fearless!

I am fearless!

I am fearless!

I am fearless!

I am fearless!

I am fearless!

You try it now...

One Step Up: You Write It!

I am fearless!

I am fearless!

Draw someone you are grateful for.

G g = Grateful - Feeling or showing an appreciation of kindness; thankful. Feels like a heart full of love. ♡

I am grateful!

I am grateful!

I am grateful!

You try it now...

I am gratefull

I am gratefull

I am gratefull

I am gratefull

I am gratefull

I am gratefull

I am gratefull

You try it now...

One Step Up: You Write It!

I am grateful!

I am grateful!

Draw something that makes you happy.

H h = Happy - Satisfied, content with life. Feeling pleasure and joy in ones heart no matter the circumstances.

I am happy!

I am happy!

I am happy!

You try it now...

I am happy!

I am happy!

I am happy!

I am happy!

I am happy!

I am happy!

I am happy!

You try it now...

One Step Up: You Write It!

I am happy!

I am happy!

Draw something that makes you more intelligent.

Adult read to chilld: I i = Intelligent - Having or showing a high level of intelligence.

I am intelligent!

I am intelligent!

I am intelligent!

You try it now...

I am intelligent!

I am intelligent!

I am intelligent!

I am intelligent!

I am intelligent!

I am intelligent!

I am intelligent!

You try it now...

One Step Up: You Write It!

I am intelligent!

I am intelligent!

I am intelligent!

Draw yourself in a jovial mood.

Adult read to chilld: J j = Jovial - A cheerful and friendly mood.

I am jovial!

I am jovial!

I am jovial!

You try it now...

I am jovial!

I am jovial!

I am jovial!

I am jovial!

I am jovial!

I am jovial!

You try it now...

One Step Up: You Write It!

I am jovial!

I am jovial!

Draw yourself being kind to an animal.

Adult read to chilld: K k = Kind - Having or showing a friendly, generous and considerate nature.

I am kind!

I am kind!

I am kind!

You try it now...

I am kind!

I am kind!

I am kind!

I am kind!

I am kind!

I am kind!

I am kind!

You try it now...

One Step Up: You Write It!

I am kind!

I am kind!

Draw someone you love.

I am loved!

I am loved!

I am loved!

You try it now...

I am loved!

I am loved!

I am loved!

I am loved!

I am loved!

I am loved!

I am loved!

You try it now...

One Step Up: You Write It!

I am loved!

I am loved!

Draw something you think is magical.

Adult read to chilld: M m = Magical - Beautiful and delightful in some extra ordinary way.

I am magical!

I am magical!

I am magical!

You try it now...

I am magical!

I am magical!

I am magical!

I am magical!

I am magical!

I am magical!

I am magical!

You try it now...

One Step Up: You Write It!

I am magical!

I am magical!

Draw someone you think is noble.

N n = Noble - Having or showing high moral qualities, having great character. A good person.

I am noble.

I am noble.

I am noble.

You try it now...

I am noble!

I am noble!

I am noble!

I am noble!

I am noble!

I am noble!

I am noble!

You try it now...

One Step Up: You Write It!

I am noble!

I am noble!

What opportunity would you like to have?

O o = Opportunistic - Taking opportunity as it comes. Accepting the challenge of new opportunities with excitement.

I am opportunistic

I am opportunistic

I am opportunistic

You try it now...

I am opportunistic!

I am opportunistic!

I am opportunistic!

I am opportunistic!

I am opportunistic!

I am opportunistic!

I am opportunistic!

You try it now...

One Step Up: You Write It!

I am opportunistic!

I am opportunistic!

What things bring you peace?

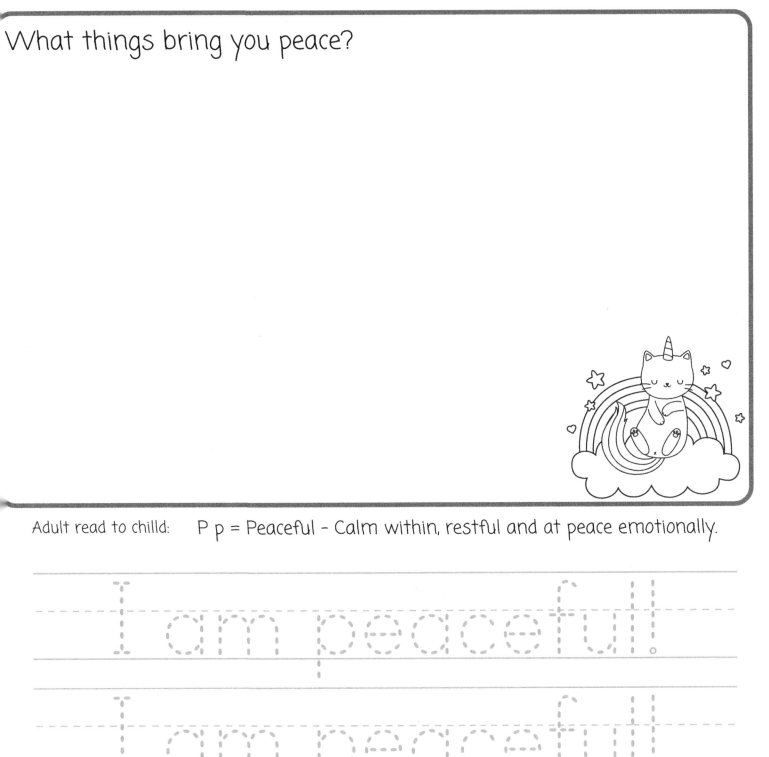

P p = Peaceful - Calm within, restful and at peace emotionally.

I am peaceful!

I am peaceful!

I am peaceful!

You try it now...

I am peacefull!

I am peacefull!

I am peacefull!

I am peacefull!

I am peacefull!

I am peacefull!

I am peacefull!

You try it now...

One Step Up: You Write It!

I am peaceful!

I am peaceful!

Draw something you have questions about.

Adult read to chilld: Q q = Questioning - Showing an interest in learning new things. Asking questions in a brave inquisitive way in order to grow ones own knowledge base.

I am questioning!

I am questioning!

I am questioning!

You try it now...

I am questioning!

I am questioning!

I am questioning!

I am questioning!

I am questioning!

I am questioning!

I am questioning!

You try it now...

One Step Up: You Write It!

I am questioning!

I am questioning!

Draw your radiant self.

R r = Radiant - Shining, glowing brightly, sending light out into the world.

I am radiant!

I am radiant!

I am radiant!

You try it now...

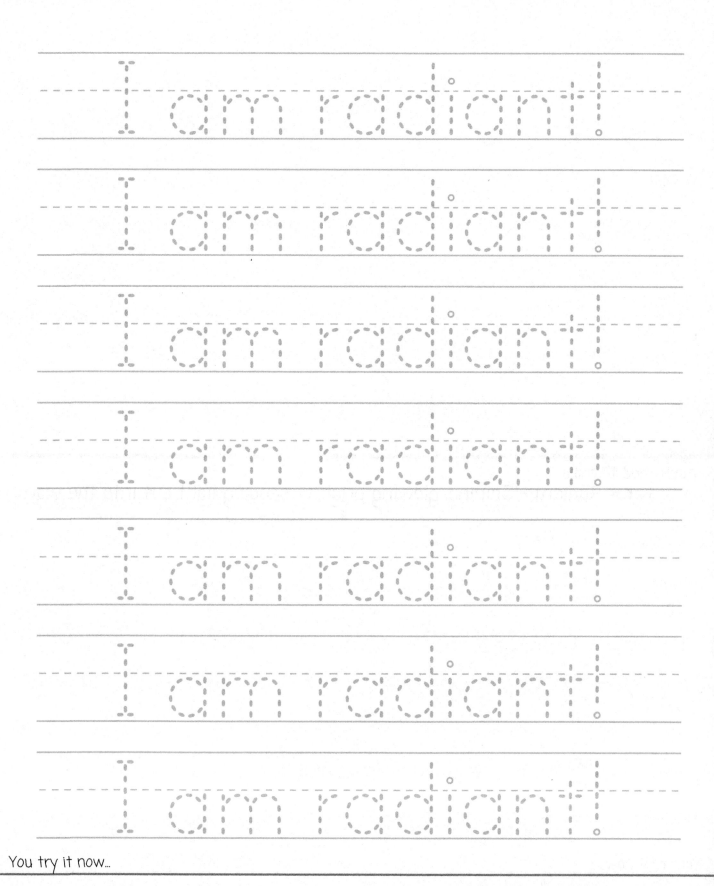

I am radiant!

I am radiant!

I am radiant!

I am radiant!

I am radiant!

I am radiant!

I am radiant!

You try it now...

One Step Up: You Write It!

I am radiant!

I am radiant!

Draw something you have had success with.

I am successful!

I am successful!

I am successful!

You try it now...

I am successful!

I am successful!

I am successful!

I am successful!

I am successful!

I am successful!

I am successful!

You try it now...

One Step Up: You Write It!

I am successful!

I am successful!

Draw someone who is thriving.

T t = Thriving – Successful, doing well in life. Healthy.

I am thriving!

I am thriving!

I am thriving!

You try it now…

I am thriving!

I am thriving!

I am thriving!

I am thriving!

I am thriving!

I am thriving!

I am thriving!

You try it now...

One Step Up: You Write It!

I am thriving!

I am thriving!

Draw your unique smile.

Adult read to chilld:

U u = Unique – The only existing one of a kind. You are the only one that is just like you. You are unique, we are all unique and amazing in our own ways.

I am unique!

I am unique!

I am unique!

You try it now...

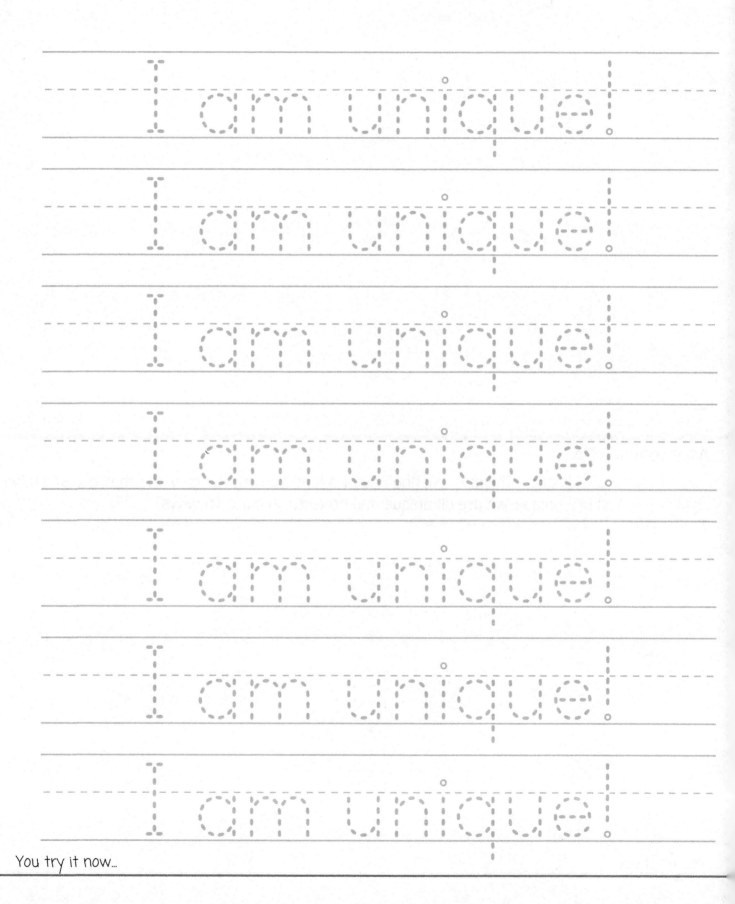

I am unique!

I am unique!

I am unique!

I am unique!

I am unique!

I am unique!

I am unique!

You try it now…

One Step Up: You Write It!

I am unique!

I am unique!

Draw someone or something that is valuable to you.

V v = Valuable - A thing of great worth, worth a lot, beneficial, of great value.

I am valuable!

I am valuable!

I am valuable!

You try it now...

I am valuable!

I am valuable!

I am valuable!

I am valuable!

I am valuable!

I am valuable!

I am valuable!

You try it now...

One Step Up: You Write It!

I am valuable!

I am valuable!

Draw your big worthy heart.

W w = Worthy - Having enough good qualities to be considered important. Deserving of respect and praise for such good qualities. Lovable.

I am worthy!

I am worthy!

I am worthy!

You try it now...

I am worthy!

I am worthy!

I am worthy!

I am worthy!

I am worthy!

I am worthy!

I am worthy!

You try it now...

One Step Up: You Write It!

I am worthy!

I am worthy!

Who do you know that is xenial?

X x = Xenial - Hospitable, welcoming of friendship and community. Kind and friendly.

I am xenial!

I am xenial!

I am xenial!

You try it now...

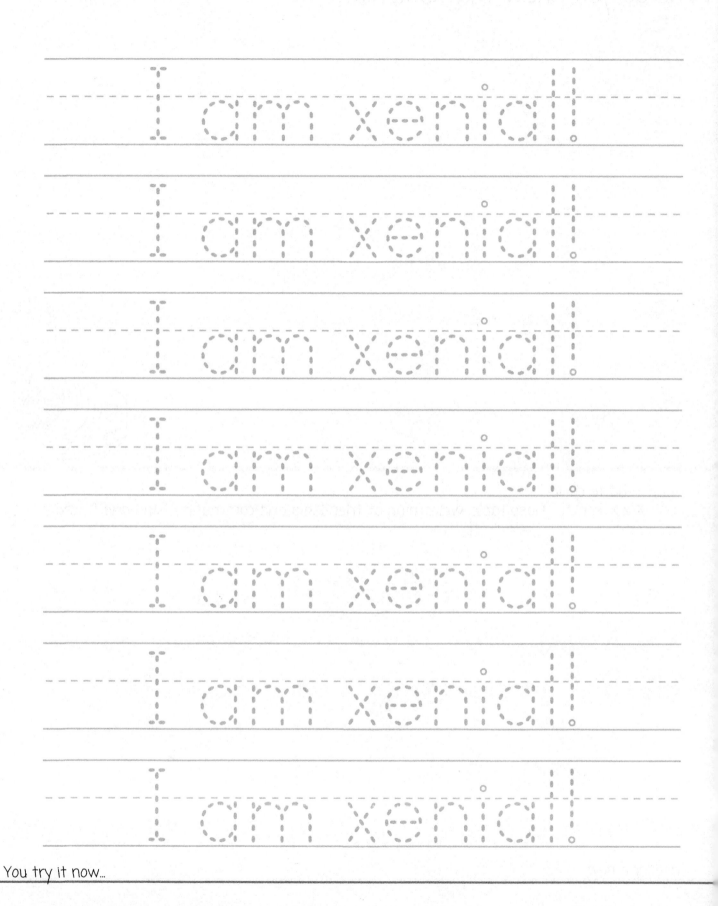

I am xenial!
I am xenial!
I am xenial!
I am xenial!
I am xenial!
I am xenial!
I am xenial!

You try it now...

One Step Up: You Write It!

I am xenial!

I am xenial!

Who do you know that is youthful?

I am youthful!

I am youthful!

I am youthful!

You try it now...

I am youthfull!

I am youthfull!

I am youthfull!

I am youthfull!

I am youthfull!

I am youthfull!

I am youthfull!

You try it now...

One Step Up: You Write It!

I am youthful!

I am youthful!

Draw yourself dancing and full of energy. Zestfully.

Adult read to chilld:
Z z = Zestful - Full of energy, ready to take on anything. Full of life and the joy of it.

I am zestful!

I am zestful!

I am zestful!

You try it now...

I am zestfull

I am zestfull

I am zestfull

I am zestfull

I am zestfull

I am zestfull

I am zestfull

You try it now...

One Step Up: You Write It!

I am zestful!

I am zestful!